Yale Center for British Art

FRONTISPIECE.
The library courtyard.

The Architecture of the Yale Center for British Art

BY JULES DAVID PROWN

Published on the occasion of the inauguration of the Yale Center for British Art
Yale University, New Haven, Connecticut, April 15, 1977

ILLUSTRATION CREDITS

Frontispiece, 1, 29, 30, 31, 32, 34, 36, 39, 40, 41, 43, 44, 46, 47—*Thomas Brown*
28, 33, 35, 37, 38, 42, 45—*drawings by Pellecchia & Meyers, Architects,* © *1977 P/M*
3, 4, 5, 25—*George Pohl*

Second edition, April 1982; reprinted, 1986, 1993
Library of Congress Catalog Card Number 82-050297
ISBN 0-930606-40-x

Preface to the second edition

In December, 1966, President Kingman Brewster of Yale University and Mayor Richard C. Lee of New Haven announced the proposed gift to Yale of the Paul Mellon Collection of British Art. Eleven years later, on April 19, 1977, the Yale Center for British Art opened its doors to the public. This account of the planning and building of the Center was published originally to coincide with that opening. Its author, Jules Prown, served as the first Director of the Center, from July 1968 to January 1976. As such, his role was crucial; his contacts with the donor and with the architect, together with his day-to-day responsibility for the infant institute, placed him at the forefront of developments. He writes as the Center's first historian, with unique insight and authority. If his account has a fault, it is that he does not accept sufficient credit for the part he played in establishing for the Center that house-style of restrained elegance which is born out of a respect for the collections.

In his introduction to the first edition of this book, my predecessor, Edmund P. Pillsbury, wrote that "it remains for the present administration and staff of the Center to create the programs and exhibitions which will integrate the Center into the mainstream of the academic life of the University." Their success in doing so is a tribute to his leadership, to the guidance of his academic advisors, and to the efforts of his colleagues within the building. They have exceeded even their own expectations. Five years later, it is not an exaggeration to claim that, with the ever-generous support of Mr. Mellon, they have established the Center within the community it serves and have propelled it towards the international prominence which is its due. The lessons for the future are clear. The collections provide us with our touchstone for action and for activities of many kinds. They are the unique resource for which the Yale Center for British Art exists. With its combination of galleries, classrooms, library facilities and study rooms, the building is designed to house a multifarious operation in which research and teaching cohabit with entertainment and delight.

Those who work in the building experience daily proof of its success. They share with the objects the privilege of a sympathetic environment in which a subtle harmony is achieved by means of natural materials; wood, travertine, linen and wool, and carefully controlled, minimally augmented natural light. In the galleries, partition walls define a series of inter-connected rooms, which recall the proportions of eighteenth-century domestic architecture. Windows allow subtle variations of side-lighting to play, shadowless, upon the walls and permit visitors to look outwards from time to time, at the Center's urban context. Within the building, openings into and across the two central courts serve a similar purpose; they provide welcome orientation and direct attention onwards, through further perspectives of treasures in store. It is impossible to imagine a more persuasive setting for a collection of paintings. In pleasing contrast, sections of the third floor are enclosed to satisfy the most stringent requirements for the exhibition of light-sensitive objects. The study areas on the second floor cater no less effectively to different, well-defined needs. As I know from personal experience as a former visitor to the Center, its Print Room offers facilities which are second to none for the examination of watercolours, prints and drawings, rare books, manuscripts and miniatures. By the provision of large tables and well-lit desks in areas ample with purpose-built storage, the building accommodates both the hunter and his prey, for that most amiable of all sports, the pursuit of images. The Reference Library is a complementary resource for students of British Art, with its basic stock of standard texts and with an expanding photographic archive which provides the visual basis for the projected census of British Art in American collections. To all of this must be added the various public spaces which the building contains: at one end of the scale, its two covered courts, for entrance, assembly and gatherings of many kinds and the auditorium with over two hundred seats; at the other, a series of more intimate classrooms and offices to accommodate smaller meetings, seminars, administration and individual research.

Such a brief catalogue of the building's practical virtues serves merely to introduce the account which follows. It is not surprising that a significant number of visitors to the Center are students of architecture; what is less usual is for the occupants of a building to be unqualified in their daily appreciation several years after its entry into service. The Yale Center for British Art is, as these pages show, a happy example of effective collaboration between patron, client and architect. The reputation of the late Louis I. Kahn rides high and, as Professor Prown points out, it is intimately bound up with Yale. The University Art Gallery, on the north side of Chapel Street, was Kahn's first important public commission; the Yale Center for British Art, on the south side, proved to be, unexpectedly and tragically, his last. This book is as relevant to the charting of that distinguished architectural career as it is to the early chronicle of the Center. It is reprinted, five years after the original publication, to meet a continuing demand.

The Center's debt to Professor Prown is compounded by the help and advice he continues to provide. He was assisted originally in the preparation of the text by Jack Perry Brown, the former Art Reference and Photograph Archive Librarian at the Center. Photographs are credited elsewhere, but especial mention is to be made of Thomas Brown, who took many of them under difficult conditions, whilst the installation of the collections was in progress. Howard Gralla was responsible for the design of the book and for supervising the production of the first edition. For his services in connection with this second edition, he deserves our thanks, as do my colleague Constance Clement and the staff of the University Printing Service.

Duncan Robinson
Director

The Architecture of the Yale Center for British Art

Introduction

This essay is a brief account of the architecture of the Yale Center for British Art (FIGURE I), its design and the circumstances of its building. The British Art Center has, inescapably, particular significance as the final building designed by the noted twentieth century American architect, Louis I. Kahn. It stands across the street from Kahn's first major building, the Yale University Art Gallery. When Kahn died on March 17, 1974, the British Art Center had been under construction for one and one half years. Completion of the building was supervised by Pellecchia and Meyers, successor architects.

More important than the British Art Center's historical role as Kahn's last building is its own architectural distinction. With its regular features and clear articulation of structure, the Center possesses a classical serenity. But like classical architecture at its best, it projects an individual presence. Although the building is strong, it achieves its distinction by modest and subtle means—perfect proportions, sensitively matched materials, honest expression of structure. It is independent, yet sympathetic to its varied architectural neighbors. It is respectful of the urban character of its setting, with shops bordering the sidewalk at ground level and an open entrance portico at the corner which allows the street to reach into the building. From the exterior, glimpses through the windows, the interruption of the stainless steel drips and concrete beams on three sides, and the splash of daylight seen in a courtyard beyond the glass entrance doors suggest the magic of the interior spaces.

FIGURE I
Yale Center for British Art.
View from the northeast.

11

Background

During the last fifteen years Paul Mellon, Yale '29, has assembled what is generally considered to be the finest collection of British art, private or public, outside of England. Whereas earlier collectors tended to concentrate on large formal portraits, Mr. Mellon acquired a broad range of representations of British life and British scenery—landscapes, seascapes, sporting paintings, informal conversation pieces, town and city views, and genre scenes of everyday activity, as well as portraits.

A large exhibition of Mr. Mellon's British art was presented at the Yale University Art Gallery in the spring of 1965. The following year Mr. Mellon offered to give his collection to Yale along with funds to acquire property, construct a building to house the collection, and endow its support. A site was purchased on Chapel Street across from the Art Gallery, and in December, 1966 the proposed Mellon gift was announced by President Kingman Brewster of Yale and Mayor Richard C. Lee of New Haven.

A committee chaired by Professor Louis L. Martz met throughout the following year to draw up plans for a British Art Center that would make optimum use of the Mellon collection to enhance the academic, intellectual and cultural life of the University. I was named Director of the Center in 1968.

The Choice of an Architect

My first task was to advise President Brewster on the choice of an architect. Much of the academic year 1968/69 was devoted to travel, consultation, reading and determining general architectural considerations. I presented the following preliminary thoughts on architecture to President Brewster in January 1969:

> The architecture of the Paul Mellon Center for British Art and British Studies[1] should be consistent with the collection of British art that is the heart of the Center. British art is extraordinarily reflective of the society that produced it, suffused with those values that have characterized life in England and in those societies that Englishmen have helped to establish throughout the world. It is an art of places, and human activities. It relates to the real world, and what goes on there. The Mellon Center must be informed by a similar concern with

[1] The name was changed to the Yale Center in 1974 at the request of Mr. Mellon, who hoped that the change would encourage broader support for the Center in future years. [By vote of the Corporation 'British Studies' was dropped from the title in September, 1976 to clarify the responsibilities and function of the Center within the academic structure of the University.]

people and with life. Rather than a pure abstract statement of architectural form, its building must relate to the people who will use it. In a word, the building must be humanistic, especially in order that the understanding and response of the museum visitor to British art be enhanced by his own life experience while viewing it.

The requirement imposed by the art collection that the building be humanistic is reasserted by the two other primary determining factors controlling the program of the Center, its relationship to the University and its relationship to the City. The architect of the Center must be concerned not only with the specific design of the building but also the broader university and urban context into which it will fit. He must consider the horizontal flow of students across Chapel Street, especially from the Art Gallery, the Art Library and the Art History areas, and the physical movement of art objects between the Mellon Center and the Yale University Art Gallery for purposes of conservation, special exhibition, study, etc. Similarly he must consider the vertical flow of vehicular and pedestrian traffic along Chapel Street; the possible disruption of the commercial life of the city on both sides of a main artery; the problems of parking, and of shipping and receiving.

The arts at Yale are concentrated in the vicinity of the Mellon Center site. Immediate neighbors are the Art Gallery (exhibitions), the University Theater (performances), the University Press (scholarly publication), and academic departments in the history and practice of art, architecture and drama (teaching). Commercially, an increasing number of fine apparel stores, specialty gift shops, book stores, restaurants, and other pleasurable enterprises are clustered in the immediate vicinity. There is an obvious and important opportunity at hand to contribute substantially through the design of the Mellon Center to making this area of Yale and New Haven humane, delight-filled and life enhancing. Such an environment would be congenial to the humanistic program that must inform the Center for British Art and British Studies.

A. *The Building*

1. *Scale*

   The building should not awe or overwhelm by its monumentality. It should welcome the visitor, arouse his interest and curiosity, evoke a desire to enter. The scale should relate to the collections, which include many small paintings, watercolors and drawings. There are some large objects. The requirements for large and small spaces, high and low spaces, public and private spaces, offer possibilities for variety. Open mezzanines, for example, may be useful.

2. *Light*

   Daylight is desirable in the exhibition galleries for paintings, curatorial offices and conservation areas. Artificial or filtered light (removing ultra-violet rays) is required for areas where prints, drawings and rare books will be exhibited and used. Occasional views of the outside world, whether courtyard or city, add variety and refreshment.

3. *Comfort*

Fatigue is the deadly enemy of a rewarding museum visit. Variety of light, spaces, scale and views, as discussed above, will add interest and help alleviate fatigue. A clear relationship of architectural parts so that the visitor retains his orientation and can exercise choice in his movements (as in a plan that revolves around a courtyard or courtyards) is advantageous. There should be ample seating in the galleries, perhaps with alcoves for conversation. A rest area which offers a place to sit, have a cup of tea or coffee, think, read, or look out the window, may be particularly desirable.

4. *Material*

The character of the collections of British art suggests the inappropriateness of brutal, rough-textured sheathings; of fanciful gossamer screens; or of cold, sheer, impersonal glass and steel surfaces. In terms of English Romantic art theory, perhaps it might be said that the building should be 'Beautiful' rather than 'Sublime' or 'Picturesque.'

5. *Program*

A primary requirement of the program, unusual enough to merit early attention, is flexibility in the scholarly use of the collections. Objects in storage areas must be not only accessible for study *in situ*, but available for easy comparative study with other material in gallery or classroom situations. Novel solutions for the juxtaposition of gallery, storage, classroom and library spaces may be required.

Subsequently, I recommended to President Brewster the appointment of Louis Kahn as architect. This appointment was approved by the Corporation and announced in the autumn of 1969. At that time I wrote:

"Louis Kahn is, in my opinion, the greatest American architect of our time, uniquely equipped to respond to the opportunity afforded Yale and New Haven by Paul Mellon's gift. He is a remarkable human being, sensitive both to the inner world of art and the external world of everyday existence. . . .

"Kahn's previous accomplishments suggest that he will create a building that will be strong and positive, but not monumental. He is a friend of daylight, and a master at introducing it wherever the program requires. He knows the visual refreshment afforded [art museum visitors] by views of the real world and by spatial variety. . . .

"Kahn has a highly developed urban sense, honed by considerable experience in urban planning. In the present instance, he is intimately familiar with the site for the Center, located directly across the street from the Art Gallery he built over fifteen years ago and . . . where he taught."

The Program

The planning committee report had underlined two primary functions for the projected Center. It was, in the first instance, to be a place where the Mellon collection would be presented "in such a manner that the significance of British art may be fully appreciated by all those concerned with the study and viewing of works of art." Secondly, the collection should be available for a broad range of British studies, serving not only as a resource for the enlarged understanding of Anglo-American civilization, but also as "a model or nucleus for developing a total view of the interrelationships of art, literature, and society."

The architect was given a program which called for a building of 147,000 square feet, containing ample exhibition space for paintings, watercolors and drawings; rare book and research libraries; a photographic archive; a print room; conservation laboratories for paintings and paper; a photography studio; a large lecture hall; and a variety of seminar rooms, studies for visiting scholars, offices and work areas. The program also included commercial space within the project. This innovation had been suggested from various quarters during early discussions about the project, and was enthusiastically endorsed by Louis Kahn. The presence of shops would enhance the vitality of the street, and would generate tax revenue that would make the project more desirable from the point of view of the city. Once it became established that shops could be accommodated without compromising the basic museum function of the Center, the proposal received universal support.

The First Project

When architectural planning began, it was assumed that the development of a design would take fifteen to eighteen months, construction two years, and that the Center would open in the fall of 1973. This goal, of course, was not realized.

Kahn began work on the project in the early autumn of 1969. As a first step he and I together looked at Mr. Mellon's collection in Washington, D. C. and

Upperville, Virginia. Many of the paintings were in storage, others hung in a house at 3055 Whitehaven Street in Washington (which served as curatorial headquarters for the painting collection), and most of the rare books, sporting paintings and drawings were in the "Brick House" on Mr. Mellon's farm in Virginia. Kahn and I also spent some time at the Phillips Gallery discussing the singularly successful relationship between space, people and art achieved there as a model toward which the Center, despite its larger scale, might aspire.

Something should be said here about the way in which Kahn proceeded to develop a plan. First, he immersed himself in the program, not so much through reading it as through discussion with the client. He sought to understand the essence of the projected building. Kahn differentiated himself from other architects by saying he was "premise-minded" rather than "solution-minded." His method was to eliminate peripheral or transitory considerations, which he called "circumstantial," in order to get back to first principles. Indeed, as Kahn put it, he wanted to get back not to the number one but to the number zero.

Kahn's greatest gift, I believe, was his remarkable ability to grasp, almost to feel, the most elemental aspect of a problem. His sometimes startling and memorably expressed understanding of the nature of man and materials, their attributes, requirements and limitations, seemed to derive from an intuitive sense of the primal. The true architect, in Kahn's view, does not create a solution, he discovers it. For example, Kahn defined the essence of a school as follows: "Schools began with a man under a tree who did not know he was a teacher discussing his realization with a few who did not know they were students."[2] That, in Kahn's mind, was the irreducible Idea of a school, the essence of every school regardless of whether it was a kindergarten or a university. And in planning a building in which teaching would take place, Kahn sought to develop special spaces, with a quality as if tree-sheltered, where people would want to stop and talk; where information would be exchanged and ideas developed in conversation.

Kahn seemed to grasp what became for him the essence of the Yale Center in April, 1969, even before he was selected as architect, during a breakfast at La Jolla, California with Dr. Jonas Salk, Paul Mellon, Stoddard Stevens and me. In the course of an animated discussion, accompanied by lots of gesticulating and drawing on napkins, Dr. Salk observed that the essential purpose of his Institute

[2]Romaldo Giurgola and Jaimini Mehta, *Louis I. Kahn* (Boulder: Westview Press, 1975), p. 109.

for Biological Sciences, which Kahn had designed and was showing us, was the study of man through what he *is*. I said that the essence of the projected British Art Center was the study of man through what he *makes*. To me, the operative word was "makes," referring to art objects. To Kahn, the operative word or concept may have been "study" or "studies." The British Art Center, despite its considerable amount of gallery and teaching space, was for Kahn first and foremost a library, a place where art objects would be "read" and studied as well as enjoyed. This perception also reflected his great respect for books, and the warm response he had to Mr. Mellon's rare book library at the "Brick House."

In addition to a sense of the Center as a library, a place where people learn, Kahn was also influenced by his conception of the English country house as a place where halls or galleries hung with pictures are not just corridors of passage but long rooms in which people browse, sit down and talk. Kahn's early comments about the Center often included references to fireplaces, which would be focal points for conversation.[3]

Kahn's next step, after he had absorbed the program, was to develop an appropriate structural system. He believed that as every living creature has an anatomy that serves its essential functions, so does a building. First it had to have a skeleton, and whether a building had the delicate bones of a fish, the massive bones of an elephant, or the carapace of a turtle depended on the dictates of its program. The Center's program suggested to Kahn, among other things, the need for large open spaces on top for the exhibition of works of art under skylights and on bottom for parking and an auditorium, with clustered rooms for libraries and exhibition purposes in between. He therefore determined for the initial project, which was eventually abandoned, upon a vierendeel truss system whereby the second and third floors would be constructed like two truss bridges, supported at their extremities, spanning unencumbered space below and bearing an open platform above. The trusses bound the second and third floors into what was in effect two enormous beams, with columns that thickened on the second floor toward the extremities of the beams where they carried more weight (FIGURE 2).

The mechanical or service aspects of the building were similarly conceived in biological terms. The mechanical rooms in which air was warmed, filtered, humidified and partially replaced with fresh air provided "lungs," air shafts were

[3]Kahn had put fireplaces in his recently completed Phillips Exeter Academy Library. In developing plans for the Center as both a gallery and a library, his thinking was informed by his work on two recent comparable buildings, the Exeter Library (Exeter, N. H.) and the Kimbell Art Museum (Fort Worth, Texas), the latter then still under construction.

"nostrils," and other metaphors were invoked for the plumbing (circulation of the blood), electrical wiring (nervous system), etc.

Kahn submitted his final preliminary design for the Center on March 15, 1971. It was to be a large four-story rectangular building (FIGURES 3–5), measuring 273 by 185 feet, extending east-west from High Street to the Calvary Baptist Church building (owned by the University) and north-south from Chapel Street to the rear property line (FIGURE 6). The site initially acquired for the Center extended completely from High Street to York Street ("from river to river," Kahn said) along Chapel Street, and included the church. Kahn was reluctant to give up the entire site, but agreed to do so when it became clear that implementation of the

FIGURE 2
First Project.
Chapel Street elevation, March, 1971.

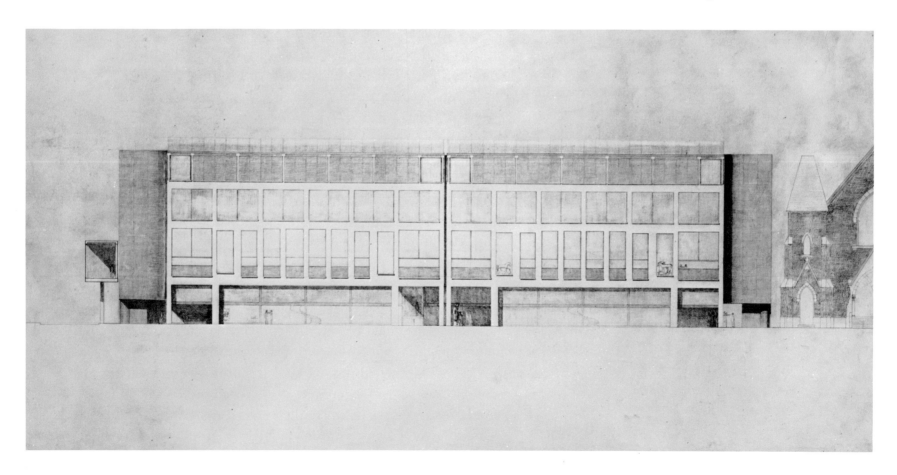

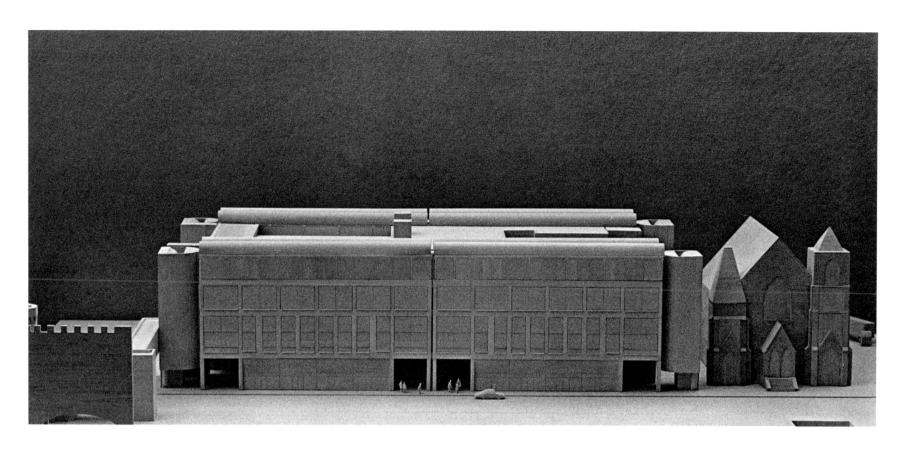

FIGURE 3
First Project. Model. Chapel Street facade.

program on the full site would have meant a long building only three stories high, the lateral extension of which I did not favor as a museum plan. Kahn was somewhat consoled by the fact that the University at that time intended to build an art library on the site of the church when funds became available. He liked the idea of a library linked by a bridge to the Center, and of course hoped to design it. Meanwhile the church was being used by the Yale Repertory Theater. Despite the fact that Kahn was delighted to have a theater next door to the Center he believed the church building itself should be taken down. He felt that it had outgrown its original function, and would eventually stand on the corner "like a dumb animal."

First Project. Model. High Street facade.

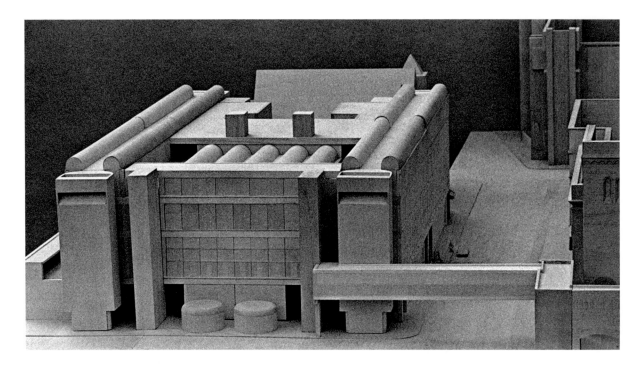

First Project. Model. West facade.

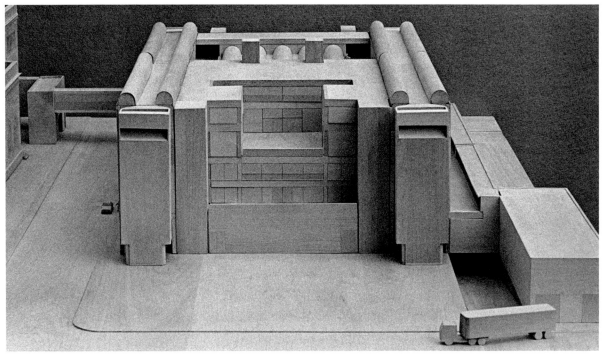

FIGURE 6
First Project. First floor plan, March 8, 1971.

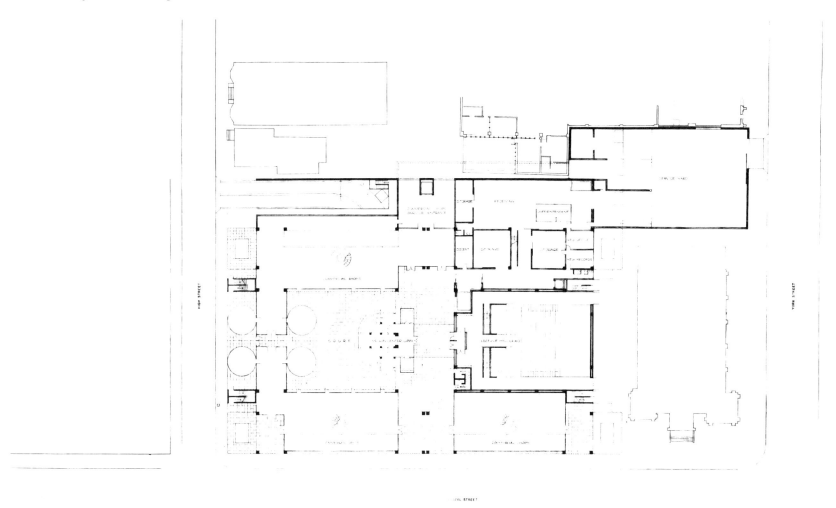

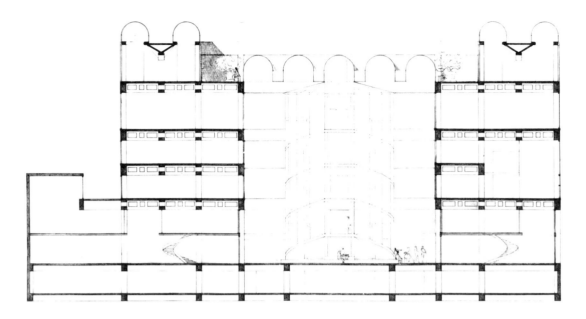

Kahn's plan for the British Art Center envisioned from its inception a building divided into two parts, each half organized around a courtyard. Perhaps this bifurcated plan was his instinctive response to the dual function described in the planning committee report and implicit in the Center's original title. In the final preliminary design the eastern or High Street half of the building had as its core a four-story skylit court around which were located shops at street level and exhibition galleries on the upper floors. The courtyard was in effect a pedestrian shopping mall, with shops north, south (a museum shop) and at the High Street end where there were also four glass and steel kiosks. A glass stair tower with a fountain at ground level stood at the west end of this court (FIGURE 7). In some of the earlier plans, the court had large trees set in concrete pockets and four glass pyramids (FIGURE 8) in bays projecting north and south from the corners of the court which gave light to a lower level shopping arcade reached by a staircase (with a fountain) at the High Street end.

A large lecture hall was placed in the middle of the western half of the building on the ground floor, with the reference library above it on the second floor and an open court ringed on three sides (open to the west) by offices on top. The main entrance in the middle of the building on Chapel Street was marked by two adjacent freestanding columns where the two sections of the building met.

Beyond these a broad interior street or passage ran through the building, with a turn to the left past the Center's staircase and elevators into the four-story court and out through a passageway between the shops and kiosks at the High Street end.

The lecture hall was entered directly across from the staircase lobby. Work areas for public education, registrar, superintendent and photographer were on ground and mezzanine (FIGURE 9) levels in the southwest corner of the building where the shipping and receiving docks were located. Underground parking beneath the building (FIGURE 10) was approached by ramp from High Street.

The second floor (FIGURE 11) and an associated mezzanine (FIGURE 12) were devoted to libraries. The combined library for rare books, prints and drawings extended across the north front. Exhibition galleries for these materials circled the east court. The reference library was in the back, but its main reading room was located in the center of the west side of the building above the auditorium with an open terrace facing the church. Daylight descended into the reading room from two glass pyramids located in the open court above (SEE FIGURE 8).

FIGURE 8
First Project.
Longitudinal section, April 21, 1970.

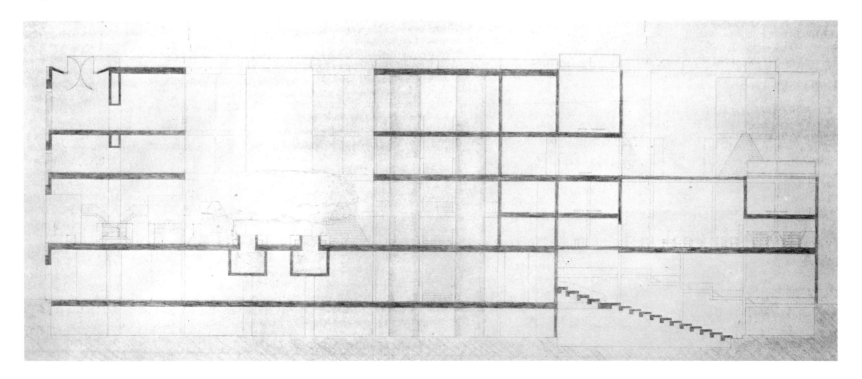

FIGURE 9
First Project.
First floor mezzanine plan, March 8, 1971.

FIGURE 10
First Project.
Basement floor plan, March 8, 1971.

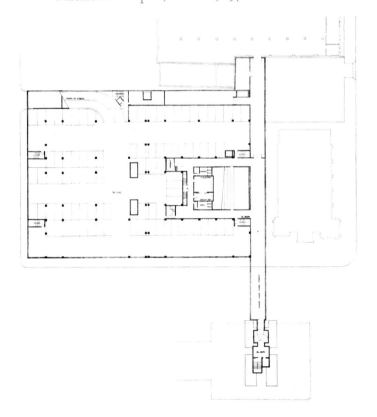

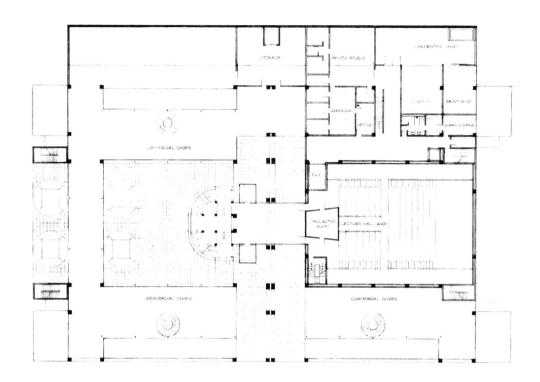

FIGURE 11
First Project. Second floor plan, March 8, 1971.

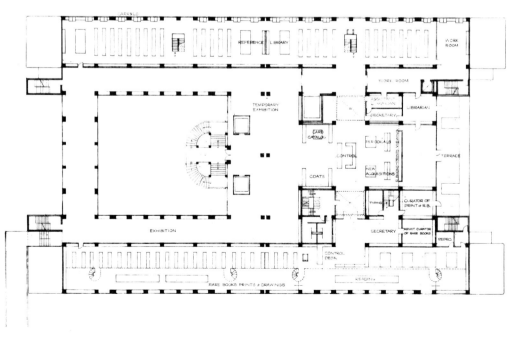

FIGURE 12
First Project.
Second floor mezzanine plan, March 8, 1971.

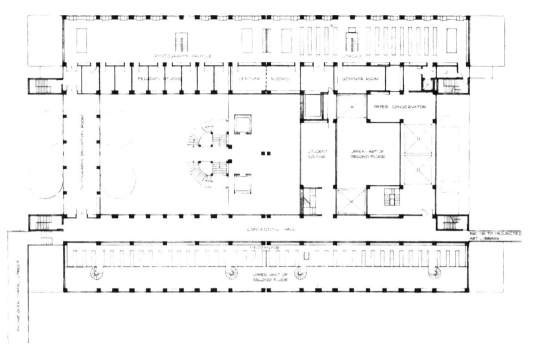

FIGURE 13
First Project.
High Street elevation, March 8, 1971.

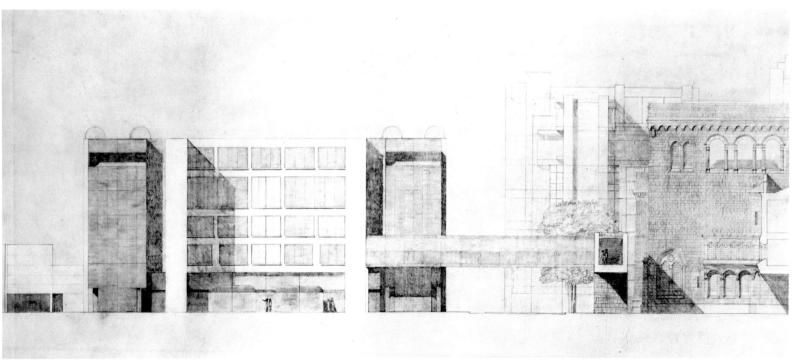

FIGURE 14
First Project. Third floor plan, March 8, 1971.

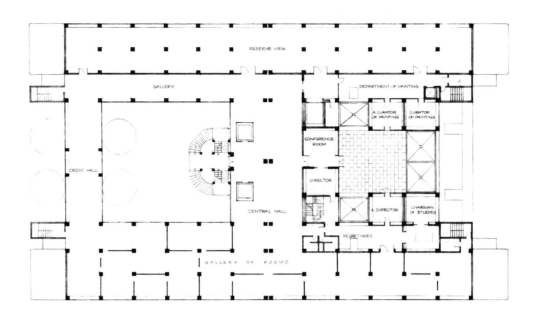

The mezzanine held stacks, the photograph archive, fellows' studies, seminar rooms, faculty–student–staff lounge and a paper conservation studio which also received daylight from glass pyramids in the court above.

The final preliminary design also included a bridge across Chapel Street at the corner of High and Chapel at the second floor level connecting the Center with the Department of the History of Art (FIGURE 13). An opening at the west end of the second floor mezzanine anticipated a future bridge connecting the Center with the projected art library on the church side. A tunnel beneath Chapel Street at the west end of the building (SEE FIGURE 9) linked the Center and the Yale Art Gallery, so that the Center's large lecture hall could serve both buildings. Through this arrangement of bridges and tunnel, the Center, Art Gallery, Art Library and Department of the History of Art would all have been connected.

The grove of columns on the third floor (FIGURE 14) within the vierendeel truss made available room-like spaces for the public display of paintings (FIGURE 15). A long study gallery was contemplated on the south side. At the west end, administrative, curatorial and academic offices surrounded an open courtyard containing the glass pyramids which gave light to the library reading room and paper conservation studio below.

FIGURE 15
First Project.
Third floor galleries, September 8, 1970.

FIGURE 16
First Project.
Fourth floor plan, March 8, 1971.

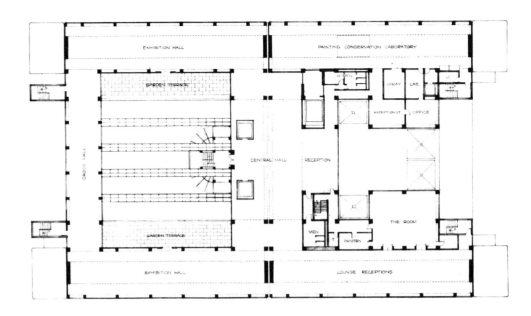

On the fourth floor (FIGURE 16) long galleries running east–west were located at the front and back of the building with a connecting cross gallery at the east end. Each long gallery (FIGURE 17), two in front and two in back, responding to the segmented structure of the building, had two skylights shaped like barrel vaults set into a flat roof. The galleries to the east were for public exhibition, the northwest gallery was a public lounge and reception area (where art objects would also be displayed), and the southwest gallery was a painting conservation laboratory (for which requirements of natural light were the same as those of the exhibition galleries). Two roof gardens north and south of the skylights above the east court could be entered from the galleries (FIGURE 18).

In elevation the most dramatic elements of the early designs (FIGURE 19) were induced by the arching skylights over the fourth floor galleries. Curved bands of glass echoing the line of the skylights provided clerestory lighting for the interior. Not only did the cladding pattern on the upper floors repeat the curve of the skylights, but even the roof was arched; the two-part building looked like adjacent airplane hangers meeting at the expansion joint in the center. However this roof treatment was rejected late in 1970, largely because the powerful architectural elements on the fourth floor threatened to overwhelm the objects that would be on display. The final design for the first project had skylights but

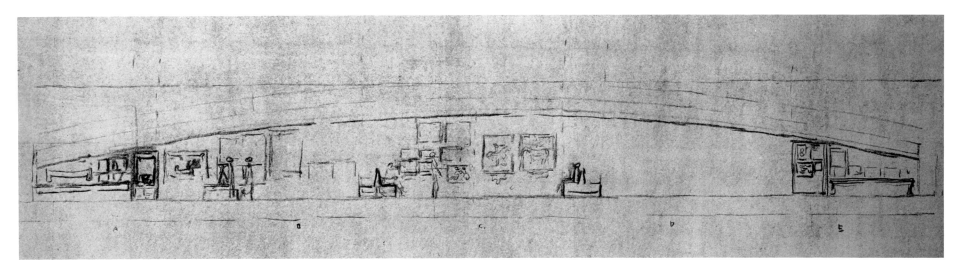

FIGURE 17
First Project. Fourth floor galleries, June 18, 1970.

FIGURE 18
First Project.
Section through fourth floor gallery, roof garden
and court, September 24, 1970.

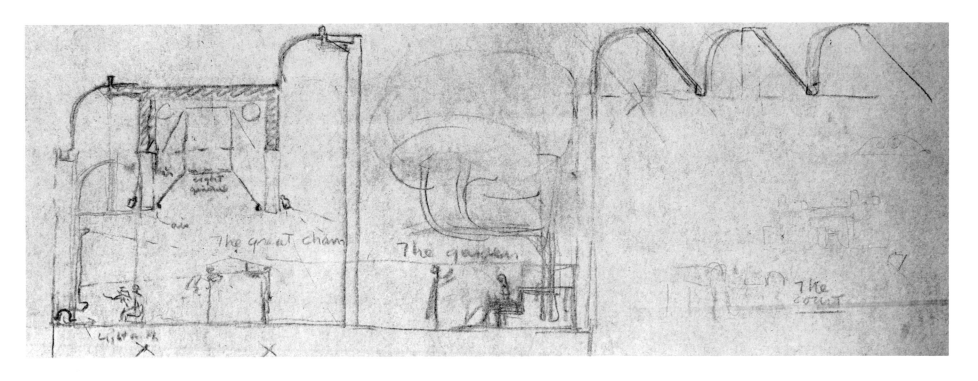

FIGURE 19
First Project.
Chapel Street elevation, June 10, 1970.

the details of light admission had not been worked out. The thought then was that the skylights would admit only north light (SEE FIGURE 18). The program for skylit galleries called for reliance on natural light on sunny and bright cloudy days, with artificial lighting required only on dull days. This differed from Kahn's Kimbell Art Museum, where natural light is admitted primarily for psychological purposes rather than illumination.

The final preliminary design of March, 1971 represented about eighteen months of architectural planning. During that time many ideas were tried out and rejected. A particularly vexing problem arose from the fact that the Center as a public institution, a museum, began on the upper floors. Except for the auditorium, the entire ground floor of the building was given over to commercial shops and non-public museum functions. Kahn had difficulty in finding a position for the staircase and passenger elevators which, as the place of access to the upper floors, assumed particular importance as the real entrance to the Center itself. Kahn referred to the staircase and elevators as forming a "medallion" on the plan. Early on it was to the right of the central interior street, associated with the entrance to the auditorium; then it was at the rear; then it was tried in several positions and configurations at the opening into the court before finally settling into a stable central location.

Certain "domestic" elements were manifest in Kahn's thinking about the building during the design phase. Mention has been made of Kahn's early wish to include fireplaces; a prominent seating area with a large glass window high up on the Chapel Street facade was often referred to as a "house;" large built-in reading room tables in the reference library were to be like rooms within rooms; terraces, courtyards and gardens abounded; and perhaps Kahn's favorite space in the entire building was the meeting/dining room overlooking the open court on the fourth floor which he called simply "The Room."

Light was a constant preoccupation—the courts and glass pyramids, the clerestory windows along the north side, skylights over the work areas on the ground floor at the rear of the building and of course the fourth floor skylights through which north light was admitted and, as necessary, bounced off of curved reflectors to illuminate gallery walls. For the exclusion of light, oak stile and rail shutters were available, folded against the sides of columns.

The Center had a freestanding column at each of the three corners of the building on Chapel and High Streets. The east and west facades were each dominated by two engaged mechanical towers (FIGURE 20). Some early elevations (August, 1970) indicated that the facade would be clad in granite panels with matte-finish stainless steel for the mechanical towers. By the final design, however,

Kahn intended the entire facade to be steel. At one point he considered the alternative of recessing the cladding to the inside of the columns, but the final decision was to have the steel and glass flush with the outside of the columns, except for the commercial shop facades on street level which were recessed.

Kahn's first design for the Center was unfortunately prepared during a period of sharp inflation in construction costs (42% from the time of Mr. Mellon's original gift). Despite the previous elimination of a second level of underground parking and a work area over the Center's loading dock, it was clear when the construction cost estimates came in that the building would have to be reduced by one third if the project were to proceed. A feasibility study indicated that this could be accomplished through substantially cutting back exhibition space, eliminating most of the reference library and all of the painting conservation department (with the thought that the Center would rely on facilities available in the Art Library and Art Gallery) and reducing the auditorium.

The Final Project

A revised program for the Center was prepared calling for slightly under 100,000 square feet, plus the commercial shops. Kahn immediately set to work on a new plan. With the benefit of the experience gained in developing the first project, the design process went forward expeditiously. Since a smaller building would occupy less of the site, and it was generally felt preferable not to have parked cars beneath the Center, parking was relocated behind the building. This elimination of the need for open space below was one of the factors that led Kahn to discard the vierendeel truss, and for the second project he utilized a simple post and slab structural system from the beginning.

During the spring and summer of 1971 Kahn produced a variety of possible plans, but rarely strayed far from the double-court arrangement inherited from the first project. Two major design concepts emerged, however, which profoundly affected the character of the final building. One was the placement of the entrance at the corner of High and Chapel Streets. In his earliest plans for the second project, Kahn moved the entrance from Chapel to High Street, leading into a four-story court as in the original project. But, probably in response to a wish expressed by President Brewster that the Center have an orientation both towards the University and the City, Kahn experimented with a corner entrance during the summer, and by fall had definitely decided upon it (FIGURE 21). A question related to this decision was whether the inner court beyond the corner entrance should be covered with skylights or left open to the sky (FIGURES 22–23). Skylights were chosen.

FIGURE 21
Second Project.
Corner entrance at Chapel and High Streets,
October 15, 1971.

FIGURE 22
Second Project.
Entrance courtyard with skylights,
October 15, 1971.

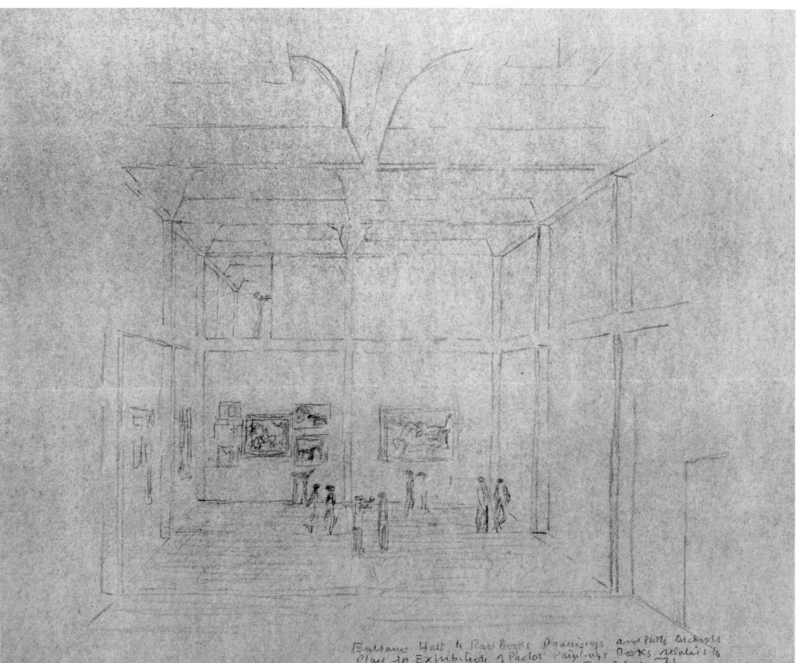

Entrance Hall to Rare Books Drawings and Photo Archives
Place for Exhibition of Photos Paintings Books relating to
Studies and general interest.   Louis Kahn 71
Light from above

FIGURE 24
Second Project. Library courtyard, July 28, 1971.

The second major innovation was a three-story court in the western half of the building, beginning on the second floor and surrounded by libraries (FIGURE 24). Kahn simultaneously removed the large stair tower from the entrance court and located it at the east end of this new court. This staircase was at first lozenge shaped, later cylindrical.

By the fall of 1971 the new plan had jelled, and most functions had found their final locations. The second preliminary design for the center was approved by the Yale Corporation at the end of 1971, and unveiled to the public at a news conference at City Hall in New Haven on February 23, 1972 (FIGURES 25–27). It was assumed, optimistically, that construction would begin in the summer of 1972, and that the Center would open in the fall of 1974.

FIGURE 25
Second Project. Model. Chapel Street facade.

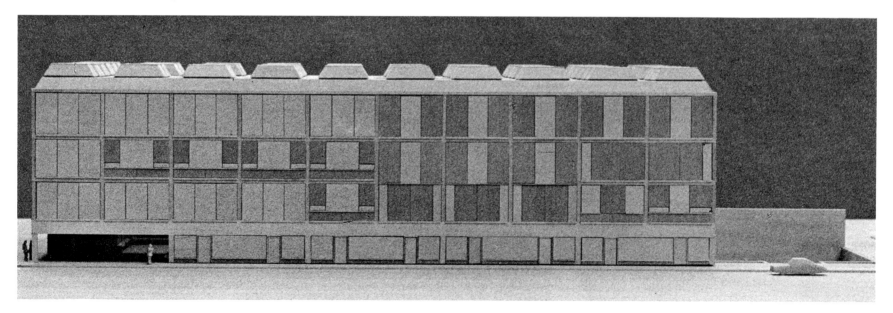

FIGURE 26
Second Project.
High Street facade and view west on
Chapel Street, October 15, 1971.

FIGURE 27
Second Project.
West facade and sunken court, October 15, 1971.

Construction

Contract drawings were not issued by the architect until July 14, 1972. A negotiated contract to build the Center was entered into with the George B. H. Macomber Company on October 1, 1972. The site had been cleared during the summer, and construction began in November, 1972. Construction cost was estimated at $7.5 million, with a total project cost, including land acquisition, fees, furnishings and equipment, of $10.25 million.

After the preliminary design was accepted, after the contract drawings were issued, and even during construction, modifications were made in the plan. Occasionally these were improvements requested by the architect or the director; most often they were economy measures to offset escalating construction costs. For example, the use of pivoting oak panels on the fourth floor, which could function either as walls projecting into the galleries on which paintings could be hung or as window shutters, was abandoned in the summer of 1972. Among other savings were the substitution of concrete block for poured concrete in basement walls, wood for stainless steel on the upper entrance court walls, and terne-coated stainless steel for Monel Metal in the roof. Major economies were also effected by simplifications in the wiring and duct work, and by the use of pre-cast vee-beams in the roof.

During the summer of 1973 special efforts were made to resolve the skylight design. A significant change had taken place in the "light theory" developed for the building by Richard Kelly. In the early schemes, the skylights had faced north in order to eliminate direct sunlight and to accept the even light of the north sky. By the spring of 1972 Kelly decided to eliminate the "blue" light from the north, reducing the amount of ultra-violet light, and by a series of exterior louvers set at varied angles and spacings to block out the direct light of the sun while admitting daylight from the east, south and west (FIGURE 28). These louvers were fixed so as to admit more light when the sun is low in the sky (winter, early morning, late afternoon) and less when the sun is high in the sky (summer, midday). The result is that the amount of daylight coming into the building from above is relatively constant throughout the day and throughout the year. Light admitted by the louvers passes through double-domed Plexiglas bubbles which incorporate an ultraviolet filter.

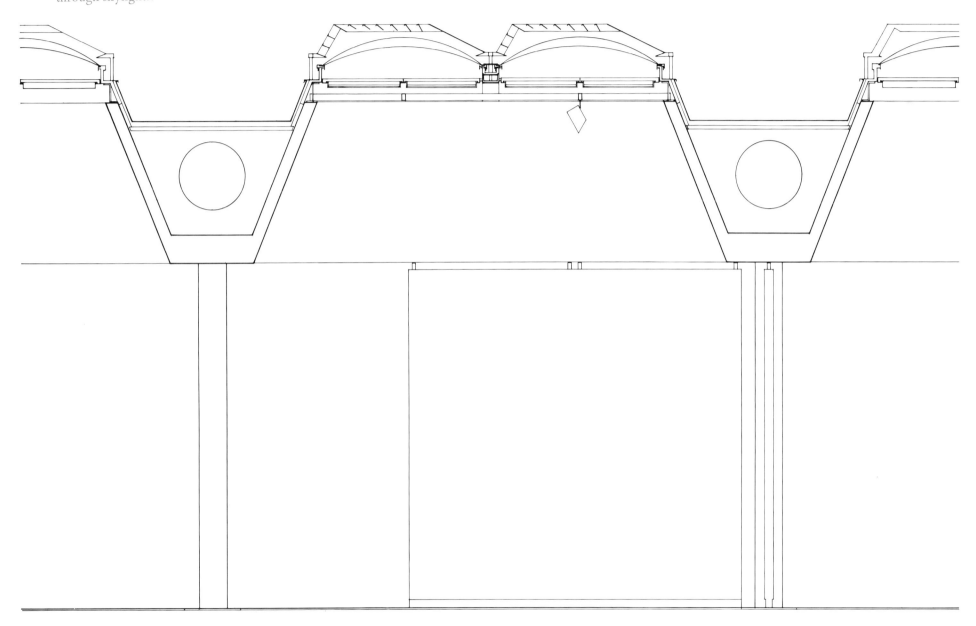

One vexing lighting problem, however, continued to occupy the attention of the lighting consultant, architect, contractor and client for several years. This was how to diffuse and redistribute the light after it entered the building. Various solutions were tested, first in a full-scale mock-up constructed at an appropriate height and angle on the roof of the Department of Buildings and Grounds Services at 20 Ashmun Street, and later in the Center itself. Early proposals by Kelly utilized a prismatic laylight above egg-crate diffusers. This directed too much light onto the floor and not enough onto the walls. Unsuccessful experiments were then made with hanging canvas baffles and with devices to shade or block out directly the light falling in the center of the room. The design of an acceptable light diffusion system was one of the few major problems that had not been resolved by Kahn prior to his death on March 17, 1974. He and Kelly had arrived at a speculative design for a prism-like diffusing cassette only a few weeks earlier. This cassette was subsequently fabricated and tried out in the building. It worked, but was so uncharacteristically complex that Kahn would certainly have modified it had he lived. Moreover it was very expensive. In the end, a cassette based on Kelly's theories, devised by the Macomber construction manager, Kenneth Froeberg, and hung according to a design by Pellecchia and Meyers was used (SEE FIGURE 46). It is very effective. Whereas sunlight entering from the southern sky through a skylight normally causes interior walls to be brighter on the north side of the building and darker on the south, the diffusing cassettes used in the Center redirect the light so that it falls almost evenly on all walls. The light is even, but the level of illumination rises and falls in direct response to the brightness of the sun and sky.

Another problem became acute during the summer of 1973. The contractor found it difficult to get a sufficient flow of working drawings from the architect's office. Kahn wanted to be involved himself in all aspects of design; nothing was so small or insignificant that it escaped his attention. On the other hand, he found it necessary to spend a lot of time traveling out of the country in connection with other commissions. As a result completion and release of drawings for the Center was often delayed, and the contractor was not getting necessary information in the field to enable the work to proceed. Therefore in the late summer of 1973 Marshall Meyers was hired by Yale to effect liaison between the contractor and the Kahn office, with the authority to make field decisions as necessary. Meyers had worked for Kahn for fifteen years, had been the project architect for the Kimbell Art Museum in Fort Worth, and had only recently left the Kahn office in order to launch his own architectural firm in partnership with Anthony Pellecchia. After Kahn's death, it was agreed by Mrs. Kahn and Yale that the interests of the project would be best served by engaging Pellecchia and Meyers as successor architects to complete the building, resolving such incomplete design details as the skylight diffusers, entrance portico walls, main stair handrail, and commercial space to the west of the building.

The Completed Building

The Center as finally built (FIGURES 1, 29, 30) is a four-story steel and glass building on a double-court plan, with commercial shops at street level along Chapel and High Streets. Developed on a module of twenty-foot square bays, the rectangular building extends for ten bays along Chapel Street and six bays in depth. A sunken courtyard to the west (SEE FIGURES 27, 37) between the Center and the Yale Repertory Theatre has perimeter commercial space for a restaurant. Parking for the public is available behind the building (FIGURE 30).

The exterior of the building is deceptively simple and somewhat austere. A basic principle of Kahn buildings is that structure must be clearly expressed. In the Center this is immediately evident in the exposed beams and columns of the facades. More subtly, the absence of exposed concrete beams and stainless steel drips at places between the second and third floors on the north, south and west facades expresses the presence of three two-story reading rooms within; the structural beams are in fact mezzanine balconies beneath clerestory windows in the reading rooms.

The facade of the Center reflects Kahn's fondness for the juxtaposition of materials closely matched in color and texture. Once, during the long design process, Kahn responded to the client's impatient query as to what the building eventually would look like with the comment "On a grey day it will look like a moth; on a sunny day like a butterfly." The image of the moth refers to the

FIGURE 29
Chapel Street facade. View from the northwest.

FIGURE 30
South facade, parking lot and delivery dock.

closely matched appearance of the dull steel and glass on a grey day.[4] The visual similarity of steel and glass on the facade responds to their linked function. The concrete frame of the building opens up the entire space between columns as a potential window. Where light is desired, glass is inserted; where light is to be excluded, the steel functions as an "opaque window." By virtue of its ability to bend, the steel itself folds to enframe the glass. In this way the glass and steel do their complementary work in the same plane, and no additional framing material is introduced.

The steel and glass are also complementary in reflectivity. On a bright day images of Yale, especially the old (1927) Art Gallery, are reflected with keen-edged clarity in the Center's windows.[5] Conversely, Kahn wanted the steel surface of the Center to be absolutely non-reflective. He often referred to the material metaphorically as "lead" or "pewter." In considering samples of steel, he would reject any that reflected his hand.

I had reservations, as expressed in my earlier memorandum to President Brewster, about the use of steel on the facade, which I feared would be cold and impersonal. I told Kahn I did not much like metal buildings, and asked him if he had ever seen a metal-clad building that pleased him. "No," he said. "But you like stainless steel for this building?" "Yes!" Despite his lack of enthusiasm for metal as generally applied architecturally as a surface material, he responded to the esthetic as well as structural qualities of certain metals (he liked metal mechanical elements to be exposed), and felt that the special working relationship of glass and steel for light admission, and the pleasing visual effect of these closely matched materials with each other and with the structural concrete made the choice appropriate for the Center.

Kahn often spoke of the facade, which unfortunately he never saw except in his mind's eye, as having a "sgraffito" effect of "writing" on the surface. I believe this referred to the pattern of grooves where the panels abut.

Access into the Center is through a forty-foot square portico at the corner of High and Chapel Streets, paved in red brick and bluestone (FIGURE 31). Passing through the portico, the visitor enters a forty-foot square court, which rises the entire height of the building (FIGURE 32). The court has a travertine floor, steel wall panels on the ground floor, oak paneling above, and clear Plexiglas skylights.

[4]The client's question reflects the fact that Kahn was habitually reluctant during the design process to make finished elevations and perspective drawings intended to show how the completed building would look. He was fearful of arousing false or incorrect expectations. He did, however, produce such drawings eventually when required, especially for presentation purposes in order to get the necessary approvals. As for three-dimensional models, he avoided detail and color, making them of plain wood with only a barely perceptible change in grain direction to indicate fenestration. Decisions about the external appearance of a building came late in Kahn's design process, after he had absorbed the program, developed appropriate structural and mechanical systems, and arrived at an acceptable plan for the physical relationship of functions within the building. Facade elevations would first appear unpretentiously as tiny thumbnail drawings in a sketchbook he invariably carried with him when he travelled, or occasionally as faint, tentative drawings in the margins or as three-dimensional projections on a plan.

[5]Kahn was quite conscious of the bold rhythm of the old Art Gallery's arcaded fenestration in designing the Center. Surprisingly, he rarely referred to his own new Art Gallery adjoining the old Gallery.

FIGURE 31
Entrance portico.

FIGURE 32
Entrance court.

FIGURE 33
First floor plan.

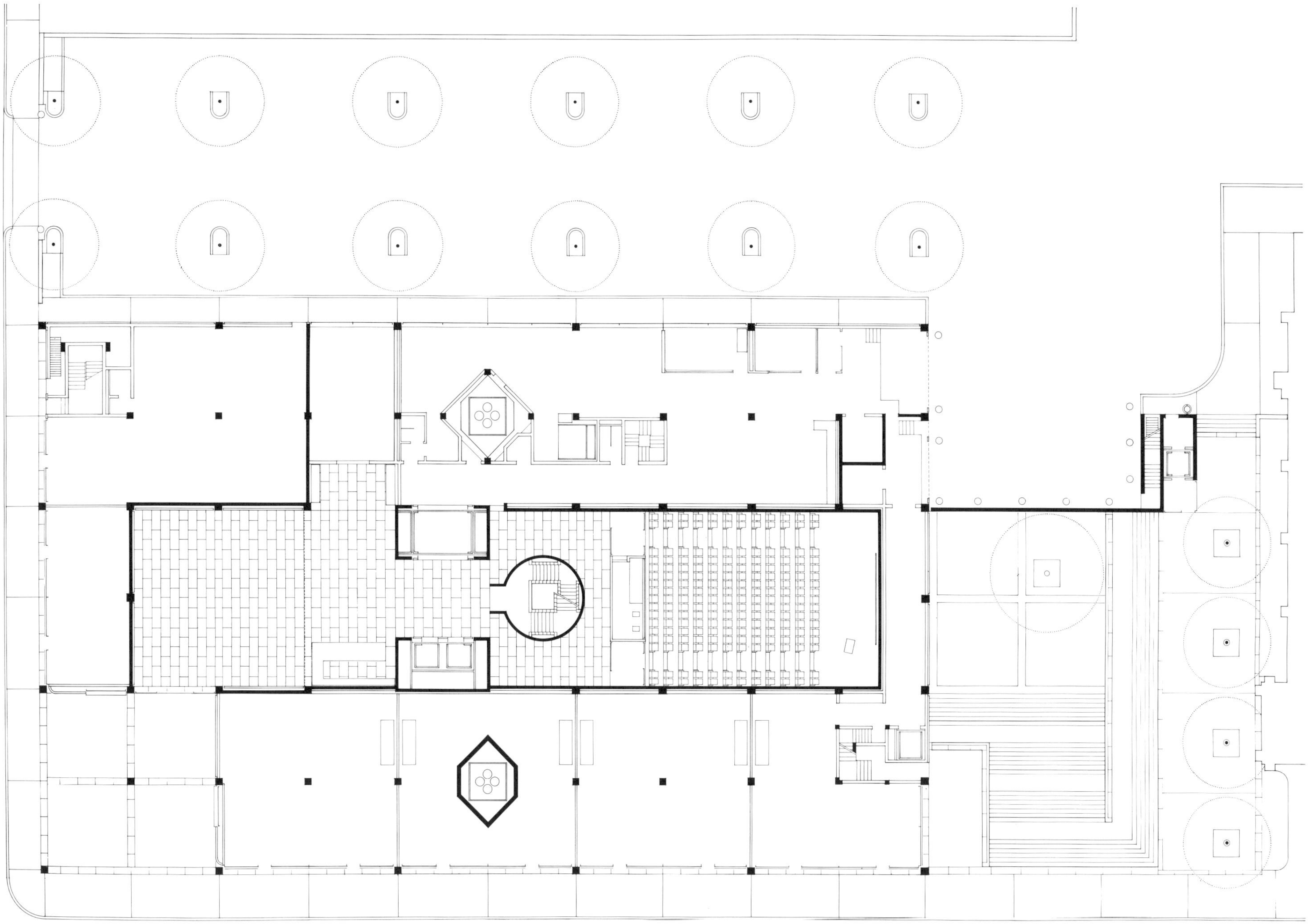

FIGURE 34
Sales desk and first floor elevator lobby.

The exposed columns, since they carry less weight as the building rises, become thinner and recede from the beam on the upper floors. Exhibition galleries surround the court on every level, with large openings overlooking the court on the second and fourth floors. This court serves a variety of functions. It is a place of entrance where the visitor's expectations are transformed as he moves from the bustle of the street to the quiet of the galleries. The entrance court is also a place of meeting and of rest, it provides daylight for the interior of the building, and it serves as a place of orientation for the visitor circulating through the galleries.

Beneath and beyond a powerful forty-foot beam at the west end of the court, the entrance lobby extends into the center of the building. A sales desk and an information center are located here (FIGURES 33, 34). The circular staircase and two passenger elevators give access either to the galleries above or to washrooms below (FIGURE 35). A large two hundred seat lecture hall (FIGURE 36) beyond the stair tower descends to the west end of the building and the sunken court (FIGURE 37).

Directly above the lecture hall, on the second floor, is the second court (FIGURES 38, 39 AND FRONTISPIECE). It has oak paneling and an oak floor, with the cylindrical concrete staircase standing dramatically at the east end. This skylit court is an exhibition area as well as a large public space serving the three surrounding libraries devoted to the study and housing of 1) rare and illustrated books, 2) watercolors, drawings and prints, and 3) photographs and reference material (FIGURE 40). There is impressive spatial resonance between the forty-foot square entrance court which rises the full height of the building and this three-story, 40 by 60 foot library court which echoes horizontally the dimensions of the entrance court.

The exhibition space circling around the entrance court on the second floor (FIGURE 41) is quite flexible, and suitable for special exhibitions where a variety of materials can be displayed. Off of this space is located a staff lounge and a small classroom.

On the third floor the exhibition space is designed especially for works of art on paper—watercolors, drawings, prints and illustrated books (FIGURE 42). A public lounge adjoins these galleries. The rest of the floor is devoted to office space, a paper conservation laboratory and library stack space around the

FIGURE 35
Basement floor plan.

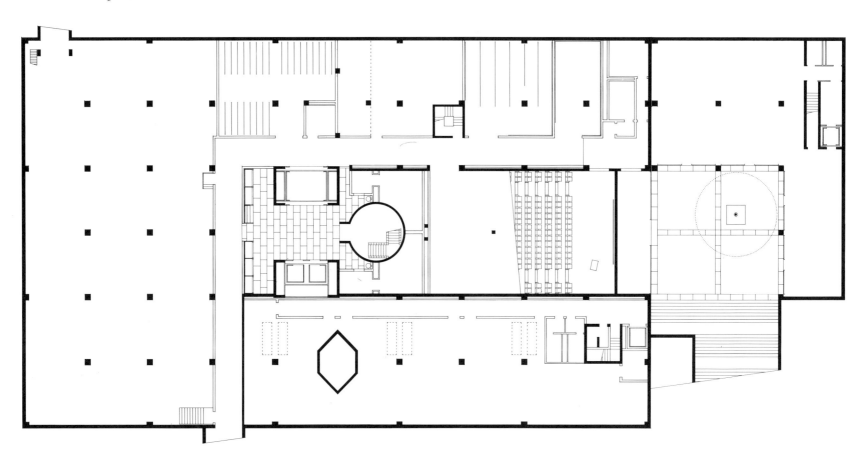

FIGURE 36
Auditorium.

FIGURE 37
West facade and sunken exterior court.

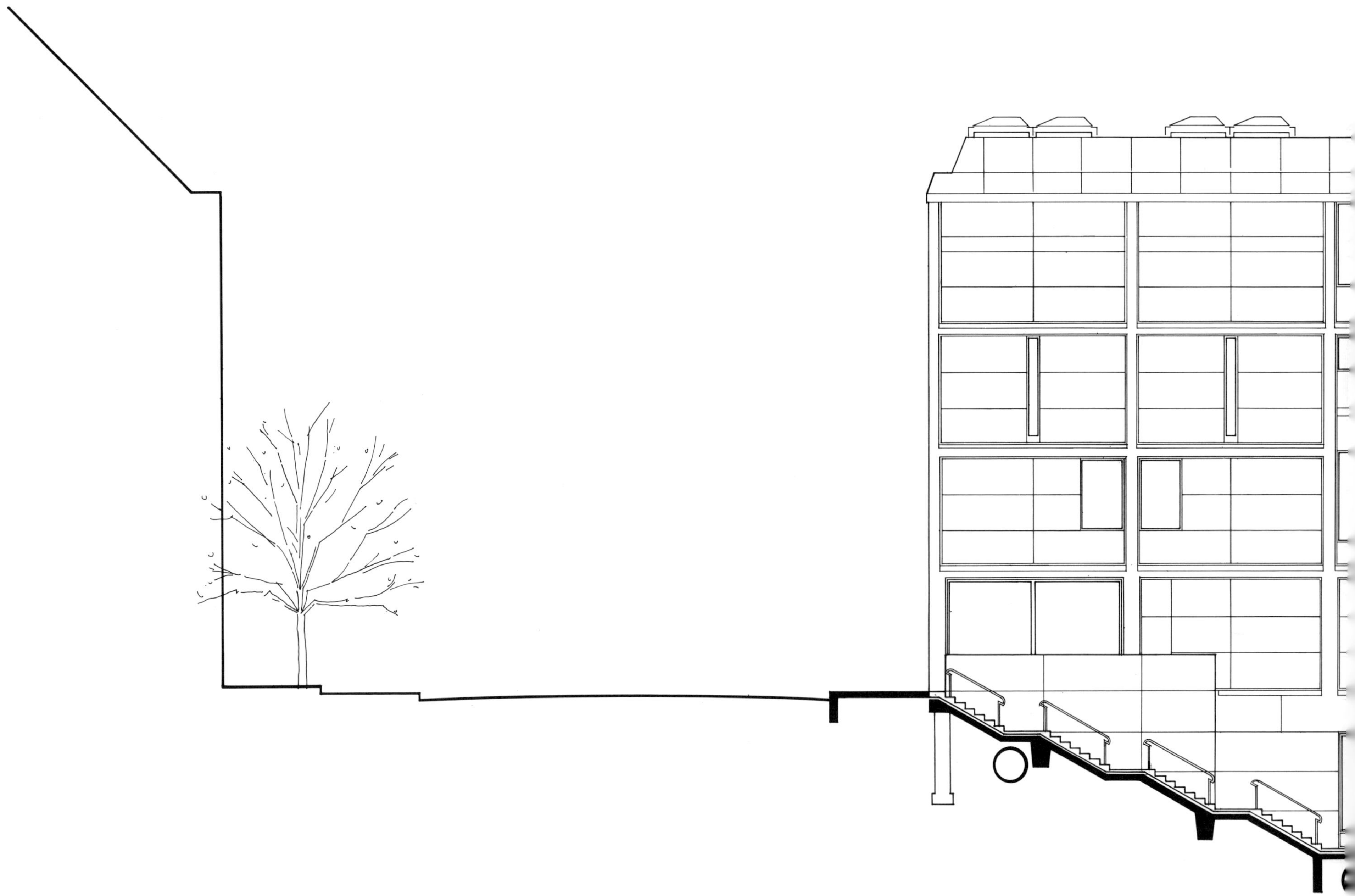

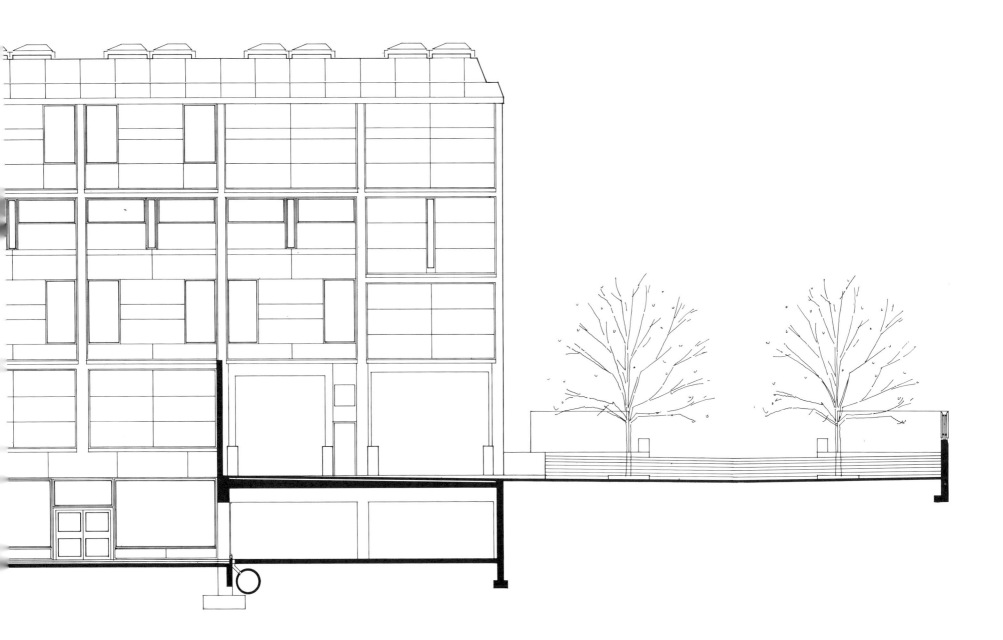

FIGURE 38
Second floor plan.

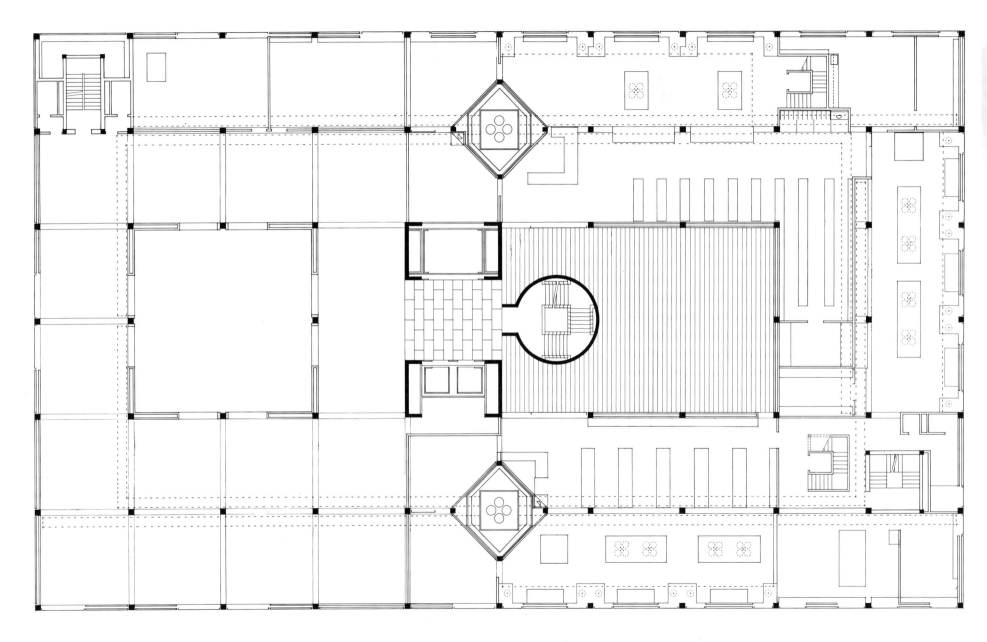

FIGURE 39
Library court and stair tower.

FIGURE 40
Reference library reading room.

FIGURE 41
Second floor exhibition galleries.

FIGURE 42
Third floor plan.

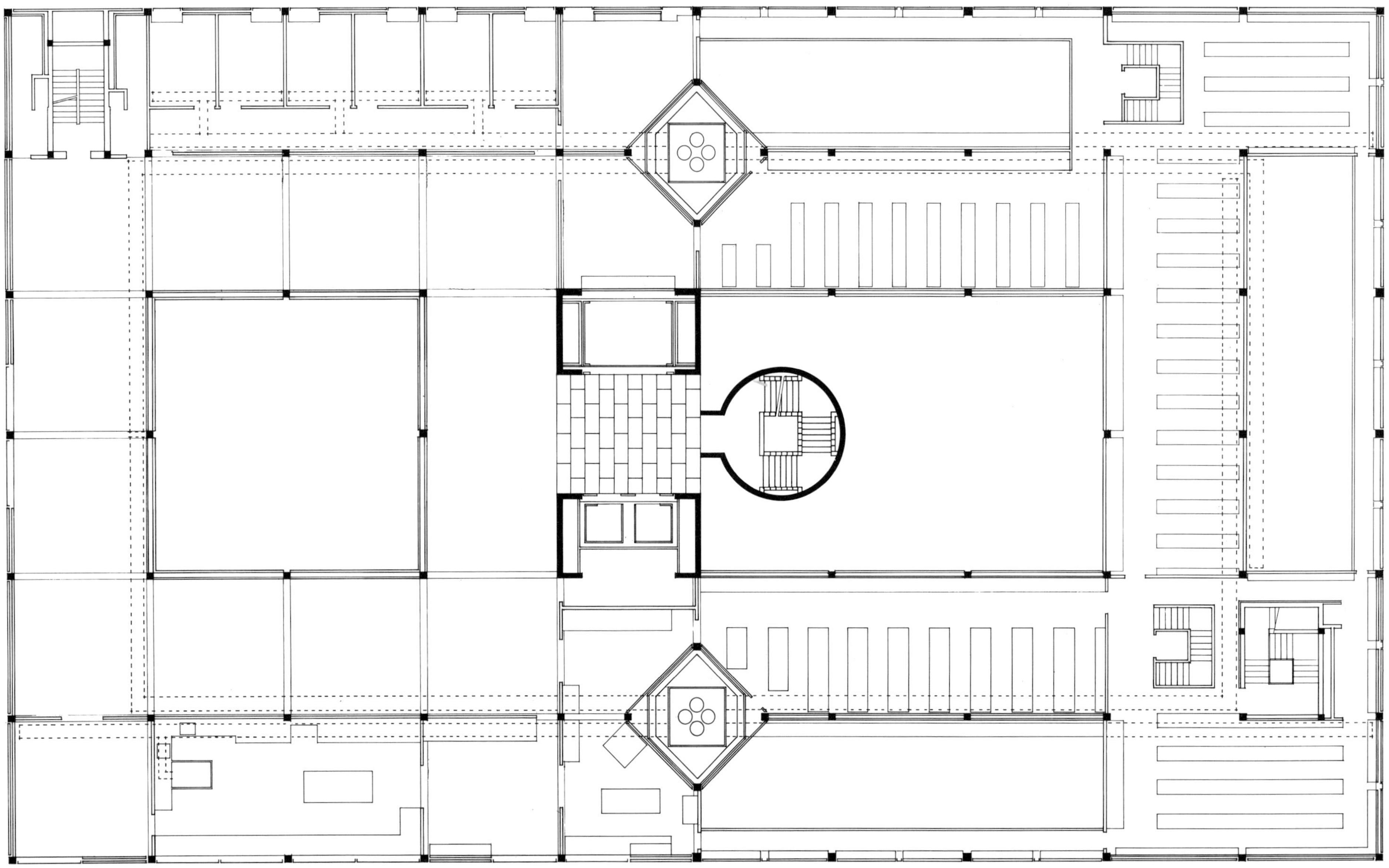

perimeter of the library court. Because this floor is devoted largely to the storage and display of light-sensitive books and works of art on paper, there are no openings into the skylit courts.

The cylindrical staircase in the library court gives access to the fourth floor elevator lobby (FIGURE 43), but does not engage the ceiling of the court. Natural illumination from the court's skylights filters into the stair tower through glass brick in the top of the drum (FIGURE 44).

On the fourth or top floor, exhibition galleries surround both courts (FIGURES 45–46); administrative and curatorial offices face outward toward Chapel and York Streets. An important feature of the Center is a study gallery along the south side of the top floor where a large number of paintings not on display in the main galleries are densely hung, available for scholars and the interested public.

The columns on each floor, spaced on twenty foot centers, are connected visually by travertine floor bands which run from column to column, articulating the structure. The concrete ceiling similarly expresses structure in bands of formwork between columns. All exposed concrete in the building (e.g., ceilings, stair tower, walls of elevator shafts, entrance lobbies) was poured in specially constructed forms which produced a smooth, almost polished, surface. The joins of the forms are deliberately expressed in concrete beads. Random discolorations, flaws or breaks in the concrete and elsewhere were not, in Kahn's opinion, to be hidden. They are, he felt, natural expressions of the way in which the building was made and should be allowed to remain rather than be cosmeticized.

The bays created by the columns in the exhibition areas can be combined through the use of specially-designed dividers into a variety of room shapes based on the twenty-foot module. Each bay on the fourth floor has its own skylight (SEE FIGURE 46) set in a large coffer created by the vee-beams which support the roof and carry the air supply ducts. On the lower floors, these ducts are exposed. In an innovative technical step, the use of "air-floors" as the second and third floor slabs largely eliminates the need for return air ducts. These floors are a honeycomb of hollow spaces through which exhaust air returns to the two large air shafts which carry it to the mechanical rooms below.

Interior finish materials in the Center are, like those on the exterior, related in visual appearance—travertine and concrete; steel, aluminum and glass; oak

FIGURE 44
Circular stair and skylight.

FIGURE 43
Fourth floor elevator lobby and circular stair tower.

FIGURE 45
Fourth floor plan.

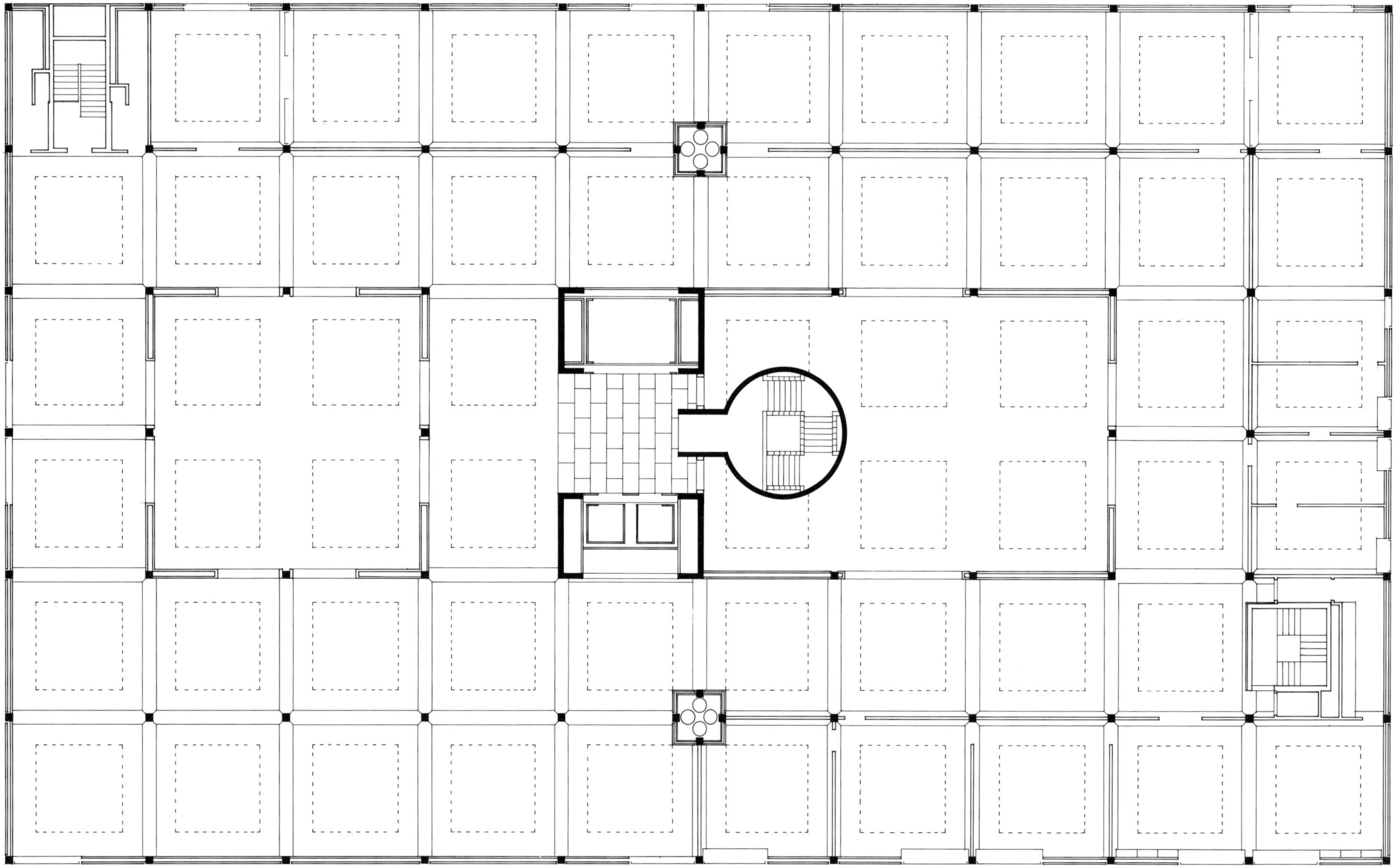

FIGURE 46
Fourth floor exhibition galleries.

and natural, undyed, beige wool carpets and linen wall coverings (FIGURE 47). Kahn used natural materials (unpainted wood or metal, undyed fabric) as much as possible, especially in the public spaces. This restrained environment provides an ideal setting for the exhibition of works of art. Each object becomes a significant event in the calm neutrality of the setting. The impact of individual works of art is especially enhanced on the fourth floor where pellucid daylight admitted through the louvers and diffusing cassettes defines each object with stunning effect.

Before his death Kahn recommended Benjamin Baldwin, who had worked with him on the Exeter Library, as interior designer for the Center. Baldwin's selections of furniture and furnishings, and their placement, respond with perfect restraint and taste to the Kahn building and to its function as a place where works of art are exhibited.

Conclusion

As a building, and particularly as a museum, the British Art Center is paradoxically most innovative where it is most traditional. An obvious novelty is the giving over of the ground level street front to commercial shops, and the Center is probably the first art museum in the world to incorporate regular commercial space. Yet, of course, mixed use buildings are common in the oldest sections of European, notably Italian, cities. The use of a courtyard plan, once a basic element in museum design but largely abandoned in recent decades,[6] is revived because it has advantages for orientation, admits light into the interior of the building, and affords the visitor looking at objects a restful opportunity to change the focus of his eyes and attention. In recent years it has been common in museums to use artificial light, which can be controlled with precision, rather than daylight. In the Center the superior quality of filtered daylight for viewing works of art is recognized and honored, and its unpredictable character is welcomed for the refreshing variety it affords the eye. When artificial light is required, incandescent rather than fluorescent light is used throughout the building. The standard preference in modern museum architecture has been for

[6]Phillip Johnson's Munson-Williams-Proctor Institute in Utica, New York, and Frank Lloyd Wright's Guggenheim Museum in New York City stand out among the exceptions.

FIGURE 47
Concrete, linen, oak, steel and travertine.

unarticulated, loft-like spaces which can be divided flexibly for various installation purposes; the choice for the Center has been to exhibit works of art in room-like spaces.

Architecturally, the building itself is original in appearance and in certain technological aspects, but its effect is of traditional, classical order and harmony. Louis Kahn, trained thoroughly in the Beaux Arts tradition, spent many of his early years absorbing the architecture of classical antiquity and of Medieval and Renaissance Italy. Yet he was also profoundly responsive to the unprecedented needs of modern man and of contemporary urban life. His work and his thought have had special meaning for and influence upon a whole new generation of creative architects. The Yale Center for British Art, in its union of the new and the old, its acceptance of accumulated experience and wisdom from the past and its innovative solutions to specific problems, stands as an appropriate capstone to the architectural career of Louis Kahn.

YALE UNIVERSITY
DECEMBER 10, 1976

Jules David Prown

Owner:
Yale University
Kenneth J. Borst, Director of Buildings and
Grounds Services
V. Peter Bassermann, Manager,
Construction Department
William J. DeBerry, Field Coordinator

Client:
Yale Center for British Art
Jules David Prown, Director, 1968–1976
Edmund P. Pillsbury, Director, 1976–1980
Henry G. Berg, Assistant Director, 1968–1973
Robert E. Kuehn, Assistant Director, 1974–1976

Architect:
Louis I. Kahn, Architect
completed after his death March 17, 1974 by
Pellecchia & Meyers, Architects

Architectural Consultants:
Pfisterer-Tor Associates, structural engineers
van Zelm, Heywood & Shadford, Inc.,
mechanical-electrical engineers
Benjamin Baldwin, interior design
Richard Kelly, lighting
Edison Price, Inc., exhibition lighting fixtures
Harold R. Mull, Bell and Associates, Inc.,
acoustical consultants
Joseph M. Chapman, Inc., security consultants
to Yale University
Zion & Breen Associates, Inc., landscape
consultants to Yale University

General Contractor:
George B. H. Macomber Company, Boston, MA
Kenneth E. Froeberg, Vice President and
Construction Manager
Theodore R. Burghart, Project Manager
Frederick P. Wales, Superintendent and
Project Manager
Robert Ducibella, Project Engineer

Site (277′ × 185′ + 40′ × 40′)	52,845 s.f.
Ground coverage of building (121′ × 201′)	24,321 s.f.
Parking area (62 cars) and delivery area	47,450 s.f.
Terrace	
Lower area (40′ × 40′)	1,600 s.f.
Upper perimeter (76′ × 102′)	7,752 s.f.

Operating Characteristics:

Temperature	74 degrees
Humidity	40% summer, 50% winter, +/- 2.5%
Air changes	6 to 15 changes per hour
Fresh air supply	20% minimum; 50% maximum
Air filtration	electrostatic and carbon
Heating/cooling	steam/chilled water from central power plant

Gross Square Footage:
Commercial space

Street floor	9,650 s.f.
Off terrace	3,821 s.f.
Basement	5,371 s.f.
Total commercial gross square footage	18,842 s.f.

British Art Center

Tunnel	1,017 s.f.
Basement	19,281 s.f.
First floor	12,298 s.f.
Second floor	23,078 s.f.
Third floor	18,541 s.f.
Fourth floor	21,096 s.f.
Total British Art Center gross square footage	95,311 s.f.
Total British Art Center net square footage	59,157 s.f.
Total building gross square footage	114,153 s.f.
Height of typical floor	12 feet
Fourth floor	
height to dome	19 feet, 6 inches
height to cornice	12 feet
Height of building	56 feet
Terrace below street level	15 feet, 5 inches

Total Project Cost: $12,500,000

Cost Per Square Foot: $108

The design and typography of this book is by Howard I. Gralla, New Haven, Connecticut

Typographic composition in English Monotype Bembo by Michael & Winifred Bixler, Skaneateles, New York

Printed and bound by The Stinehour Press, Lunenburg, Vermont

Production supervision by Yale University Printing Service